JEWELRY BY JOAN RIVERS

JEWELRY BY

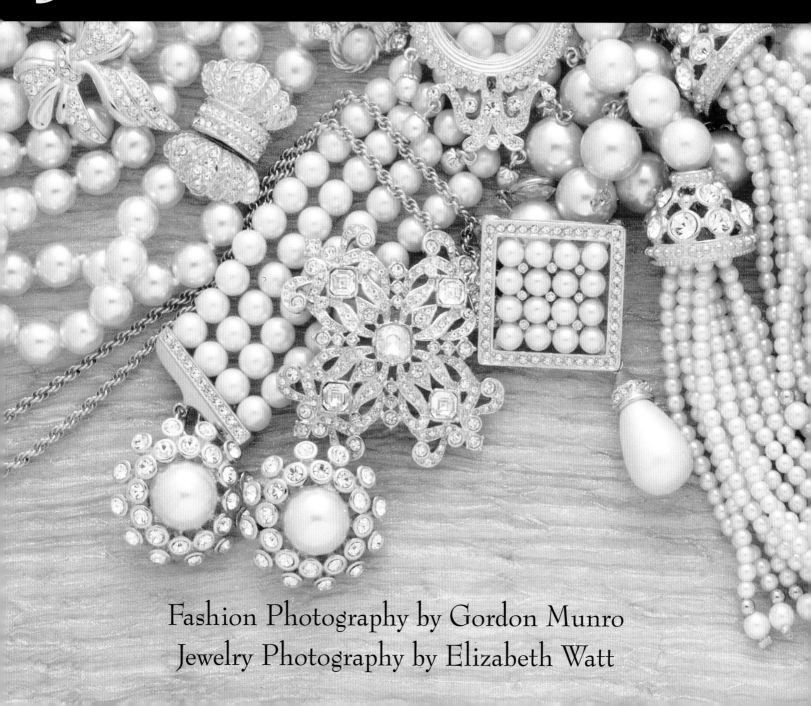

Fashion Photography by Gordon Munro
Jewelry Photography by Elizabeth Watt

JOAN RIVERS

Abbeville Press Publishers

New York London Paris

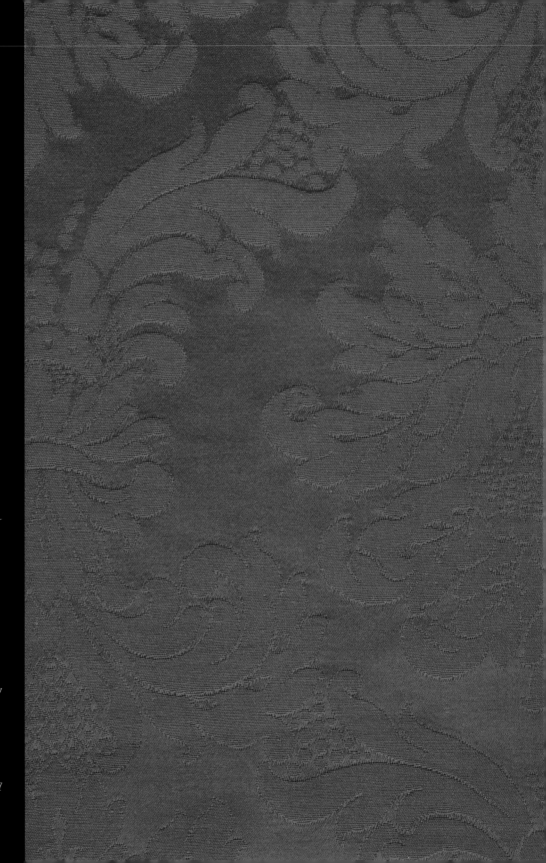

EDITOR: Jacqueline Decter
MANUSCRIPT EDITOR: Todd Lyon
CREATIVE CONSULTANT: David Dangle
DESIGNER: Renée Khatami
ART DIRECTOR: Patricia Fabricant
PRODUCTION EDITOR: Abigail Asher
PRODUCTION MANAGER: Lou Bilka

Fashion shoot
STYLIST: Angela Wein-Nilsson
HAIR STYLIST: Robert Chiu
MAKEUP ARTIST: Adele Fass-Licata

Additional photography credits
Laura Straus: pages 141, 145, 146, 148, 150, 151.
© Sotheby's, Inc.: page 37, 1994; page 45, 1995; page 48, 1994; page 55, 1993; page 59, 1994.

First edition
0 9 8 7 6 5 4 3 2 1

Library of Congress Cataloging-in-Publication Data
Rivers, Joan.
    Jewelry by Joan Rivers / text by Joan Rivers ; fashion photography by Gordon Munro ; jewelry photography by Elizabeth Watt.
        p.   cm.
    Includes bibliographical references and index.
    ISBN 1-55859-808-1
    1. Jewelry. 2. Jewelry making. I. Title.
TS725.R59   1995
391'.7—dc20   95-21217

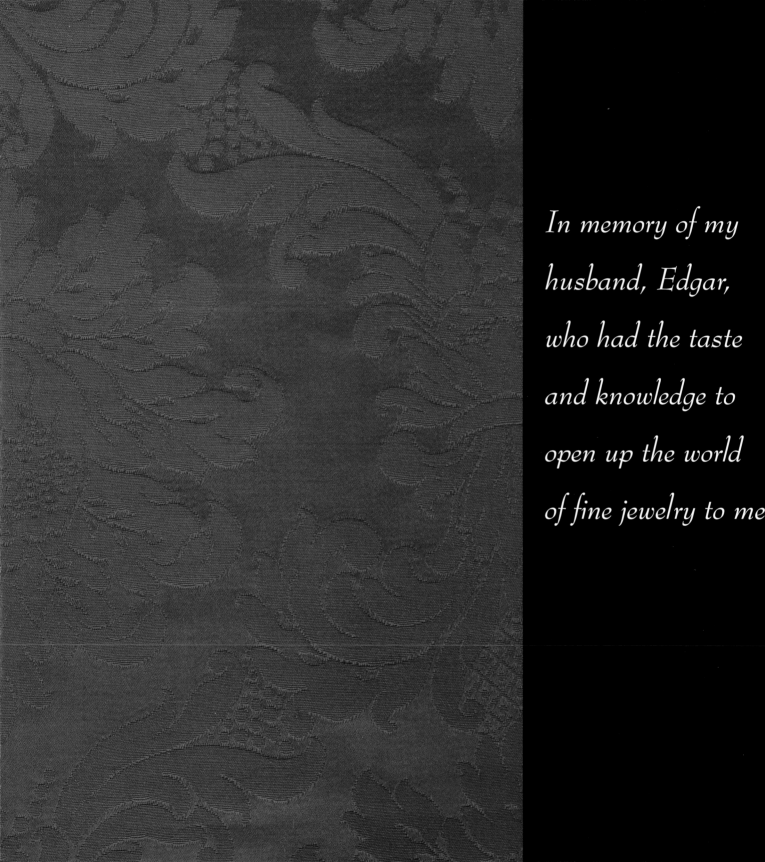

In memory of my husband, Edgar, who had the taste and knowledge to open up the world of fine jewelry to me

I have always loved jewelry. Even as a child, when other girls in Larchmont were dreaming of becoming cheerleaders or prom queens, I would spend hours drawing pictures of women, their faces framed by lavish earrings. Sketch pad in hand, I'd experiment with drops, buttons and hoops; on long necks I'd draw diamond chokers, strands of pearls, simple pendants. Rough as I'm sure these early efforts were, to me they were absolutely captivating. Each sketch was another possibility, another way for the mysterious woman of my childhood dreams to express her individuality. To me, those imaginary jewels represented not only her moods but her inner flame, her very essence.

I once read about a woman who'd taken all the diamonds she owned and had them made into one extraordinary piece of jewelry. I thought it was a terrific idea, so I borrowed it. I took an odd assortment of diamond jewelry — left to me by my grandmothers, mother-in-law, even my own darling mother — to the house of Harry Winston, and his designers created this flower pin for me. Both versions — the original on the left and the near-original on the right — feature a removable "stem," so the pin can feel equally at home on a scarf, at a neckline, or even on a hat.

Over the years, as fashions came and fashions went, my love for jewelry never wavered. I still cherish every gift of jewelry I've ever received, and I find that no matter how many pieces I may already own, it's never too much. I collect jewelry with an intensity usually reserved for fine art collectors. And why not? Jewelry *is* art.

Whether it's sitting in a cotton-lined box or draped across blue velvet in the window at Cartier, a beautifully designed, beautifully made piece of jewelry is a treasure, a joy to behold. But I'm convinced that even the most spectacular piece is incomplete unless it is worn. Jewelry needs to be cradled in the hand, held to the light, and, especially, warmed by the skin. To my eye, a jewel never sparkles the way it sparkles when it's worn by a confident woman. That's when quality and design make magic; that's the final, elusive element that transforms a fine piece of jewelry into a work of art.

And that, after all, is what this book is all about.

IN THE BEGINNING, THERE WAS STICKER SHOCK

There's an expression you may have heard: "When artists get together, they talk about money. When bankers get together, they talk about art."

Which means, of course, that you can have all the money in the world and still not have art, or you could have no money at all and still have art. *Lots* of art.

Let me tell you a story: When I started working on "The Joan Rivers Show," an Emmy award–winning costume designer named David Dangle came in to discuss wardrobe designs. (David is now my design associate.) For the meeting he brought in some jewelry, including a necklace. It was nothing extravagant, just an attractive piece of costume jewelry, a choker that he thought might work with a certain suit. I took it in my hand and turned it over to see the price tag . . . it cost $1,750! I was so shocked I almost dropped it on the floor. "Who," I blurted out, "has $1,750 to spend on a piece of *costume* jewelry?!" There was no answer to that question. I thought the whole *point* of costume jewelry was to have the fun of dressing like a wealthy woman with virtually none of the worry or expense. I was so outraged by that one price tag that it got me wondering: Does well-made costume have to be pricey? Isn't there some way, without taking a second mortgage on her home, that a woman can own beautiful jewelry to wear, cherish, and pass along?

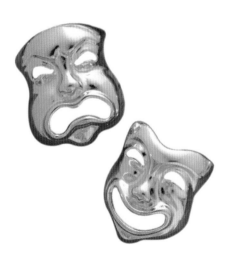

That evening I went home and started looking over my own collection. I'd been fortunate over the years because my late husband, Edgar Rosenberg, had always indulged my love of jewelry, and I had a wonderful collection to show for it. Well, I laid my best treasures out, and that night I really *looked* at my very favorites. I touched the pieces that I wore most often, thought about what I wore them with, where I went in them, how I felt when I wore them. It was a fun tour to take, and I learned a lot. I learned that within my small galaxy of jewels there were certain items that made me feel like an all-powerful queen, and others that made me feel like a wicked temptress. There were pieces that spoke of history, of worldliness. Others oozed class; they were the very definition of "understated elegance." On my visit to that land of baubles and bangles I saw wit and playfulness, opulence and romance, drama and intrigue. But there was one thing I didn't see: I didn't see any reason why women of all shapes, sizes, ages, incomes, and backgrounds shouldn't have a collection like this. It gave me ideas. I could barely sleep.

Life is a series of coincidences, don't you think? The very next day, out of the blue, a friend of mine was contacted by the QVC cable network. They asked him if I would be interested in endorsing a line of cosmetics.

At the time cosmetics didn't particularly interest me, but I let QVC know that I did have these jewelry ideas flying around in my head. After that, I started sketching with a vengeance. I adapted some designs from my personal jewelry collection, then had them produced for a price that I felt was within the reach of stylish American women who were also smart. I had to name the line, of course, and there was little doubt in my mind: what else but the Joan Rivers Classics Collection? I went on QVC and sold every last piece. It was encouraging, to say the least. QVC then asked me to design a new group of jewels, which sold out as well. After several more appearances, with the same result, I realized this had become a real business, and I knew I had to get a staff together. So I called up my old friend David Dangle and said, "How would you like to work with me?" He took to the idea like a duck to water.

The process was almost indescribably exciting. We three — David, the sketch pad, and I — came together to create a collection of costume jewelry that would be at once beautiful, wearable, and, best of all, affordable. Our plan was to explore the world of jewelry, find the very best pieces, then adapt them so they would work for real women in the real world. We're still at it, and we're having a wonderful time.

WISDOM AND PEARLS

Where does a collection begin? With the essentials, basic pieces upon which a woman can build a wardrobe of jewelry. But even among the essentials there are quintessentials, and so the very first piece David and I collaborated on for the Joan Rivers Classics Collection was a strand of pearls. Pearls! Worn by the great women of history, from Cleopatra to Queen Elizabeth. Worn by women of all ages, from young girls in white dresses to formidable matriarchs in their Sunday best. Brides glide down the aisle wearing their mother's pearls; new pearls are added when babies are born. On that special day when a woman inherits the pearls that belonged to her mother and her grandmother, the circle is not only unbroken but enhanced — and isn't it lovely that pearls, in order to maintain their luster, must be worn? Pearls work with everything; they are the very meaning of the word *classic*. And our first strand of pearls was classic, indeed: one long, luxurious rope with a sparkling clasp.

Think of the possibilities within that one piece of jewelry! The elegance of the pearls themselves, smooth beauties with the power to turn a simple black suit into a smashing outfit; all that length, just begging to be played with, to be wound into a double or triple strand, or worn freely

Peter Carl Fabergé knew his precious stones and pearls, and knew how to perfectly balance their beauty. On the left, a diamond Maltese cross dangles from a rope of luminous pearls, captured by a clasp of diamonds and sapphires. On the right, our interpretation makes an appearance in Austrian cut crystal. Unlike its older sister, ours has an enhancer clasp that allows it to be worn as an extravagant brooch.

swinging, like a madcap flapper; and that fascinating clasp. Even if a woman has worn the same suit to ten business meetings that day, she could create an evening look simply by turning the strand around so that the decorative clasp was in front. That sparkling detail would suddenly become the focal point of the outfit, making it absolutely right for a night out.

It's wonderful to own jewelry that can be worn in many different ways. After all, a versatile piece of jewelry is a practical piece of jewelry — it won't wait in a drawer for a special occasion but will become part of a working wardrobe. Perhaps more important, versatility means variety — and don't we love variety? It really is the spice of life. Columbus crossed the ocean seeking spice; we find it in a strand of pearls.

FROM RUSSIA, WITH LOVE

When I look at jewelry, I see history. Egyptian scarabs, native American turquoise, French cocktail rings: at every time and place in history, jewelry has been there, and each piece has a story to tell.

I think each of us has a favorite historical era, one we secretly wish we'd been born into. For me it's old Russia. What could be more luxurious than white nights and Fabergé, snow and gold and blue enamel? Over the years I've collected Russian jewelry, and each piece makes me feel as if I've stepped out of a magnificent painting. I have a pearl choker that was once given to a Romanov lady by her lover; a whole revolution and one Cold War later, Edgar bought it and gave it to me. The first time I wore the pearls, to an evening ball, I felt dramatic and distinctive. I carried two histories; that

This brooch, featuring a high-domed star sapphire set in a beribboned frame of diamonds, was made for the Grand Duchess Vladimir, sister-in-law of Czar Alexander III, by the house of Fabergé. If you're a student of jewelry, you'll recognize the piece right away: it's been featured in numerous books and was exhibited at the 1994 winter antiques show at the New York Armory. It was presented to me by my husband for our twelfth anniversary; he acquired it from the house of Wartski, that famous English dealer of Fabergé treasures. My newer version on the right has the same dramatic impact as the original, but definitely won't spend all its time in a vault.

unknown woman of long-ago Russia was linked to me by the enduring beauty of that necklace, and by the timeless beauty of a gesture of love.

Given my passion for all things Russian, I didn't hesitate when I learned that the first organized exhibition of Fabergé jewels since 1914 was taking place in St. Petersburg. It was 1993; I packed my sketchbook

and hopped a plane to that city, one of the most beautiful in the world. What an amazing place! Built by Peter the Great as a "window to the West," it is low and luminous, with an exquisite sense of light that comes from the pale, jewel-like colors of the buildings themselves.

In czarist St. Petersburg, beauty meant opulence and extravagance. There, the whole of the Russian aesthetic could be seen in a single Fabergé egg, and the recipe for that egg was anything but simple. Ingredients included solid gold interspersed with delicate patterns of shining enamel; perfect groupings of pearls and precious stones; and exquisite craftsmanship to make it last forever.

I returned from St. Petersburg totally inspired, with stars in my eyes and ideas in my head. The first thing I did was take out what is perhaps the most influential piece in my own collection: Queen Marie of Romania's Fabergé egg necklace.

Queen Marie of Romania was one of the most fascinating figures of the 1920s. She was the consummate celebrity, a woman of great beauty, wit, and power who traveled the world, gaining admirers everywhere she went. She was so well known and so beloved that her name became synonymous with a charmed life, as in this poem by Dorothy Parker:

Oh, life is a glorious cycle of song
A medley of extemporanea
And love is a thing that can never go wrong
And I am Marie of Romania.

When Edgar presented me with Queen Marie's necklace, he gave me an extraordinary piece of history as well as a truly stunning work of art. Imagine a knee-length gold chain dripping with Fabergé eggs and charms. Can you see it? When my daughter, Melissa, was a child, we'd lie on my bed and play with it for hours. Each time I took it out she'd discover something different — a little ivory pig, a centime coin, a piece of hematite from the World War I era, and, of course, those dazzling eggs. Each egg on the necklace is significant, and a few are engraved by Marie's husband. I wish I could ask the queen herself who gave her each egg, and what it meant to her. Though I'll never have the chance, the necklace does include a piece of my personal history: when Edgar bought it, he added a charm and had it inscribed to me in his own handwriting.

Queen Marie's necklace inspired me to create a similar piece for my Russian line. It has a timeless design that's right at home in the New

World; not only beautiful and unusual, it's utterly versatile. Each egg and each charm can be removed to be worn singly; the necklace itself can be shortened or lengthened, as the mood strikes; and the whole piece can be personalized with eggs and charms of one's own choosing. It's a necklace made for a queen, and my hope is that every woman feels like a queen when she wears it.

SENTIMENTAL VALUE

If your doorbell were to ring right now and a delivery person were to present you with a long box of red roses, what would you do? After scrambling to read the accompanying card, you'd most likely scream your head off in horror and/or delight. Because, as every American man, woman, and florist knows, a gift of a dozen red roses means "I love you." But did you know that jewels have their own secret language, too? It's true, and it was all the rage in that fancy, frilly time we call the Victorian era.

Proper Queen Victoria's reign (1837–1901) was all about the repression of one's "animal nature." High morals ruled. Corseted ladies hid their womanly charms under piles of petticoats, and the idea of exposed body parts was so scandalous that even furniture legs were hidden

Pages 22–23: This is the fabulous necklace that belonged to Queen Marie of Romania. A cascade of Fabergé eggs and charms, it was given to her by her husband, King Ferdinand. If you look closely, you can see a jade Buddha; a rooster hatching from an egg; a portrait of a boxer; and a tiny windowed egg through which a minuscule ladybug can be glimpsed. To capture the spirit of Marie's masterpiece I've adopted the unique spring-clasp modular design and created eggs inspired by old Russia, as well as symbols of luck (the clover), love (the heart), and longevity (the elephant).

under ruffles. Back then, courtship was an elaborate ritual involving gloved hands, iambic pentameter, and suffocating codes of social etiquette. With so much repression going on, it was almost inevitable that the idea of the secret message would take hold — and what better vehicles than brooches, bracelets, lorgnettes, and pendants to send intimate thoughts to lovers and friends?

To those in the know, gemstones came to represent such qualities as sincerity (amethysts), innocence (diamonds), happiness (emeralds), and love (rubies). There was a detailed glossary of the meanings of flowers (pansies, for example, meant "think of the giver"). Objects had meaning, too: the anchor stood for hope; the salamander, which was once believed to thrive in fire, came to mean passion; and a snake swallowing its tail signified eternal love. Many images derived their meaning from ancient mythology, but to nineteenth-century Europeans it all translated into personal sentiment.

Some Victorian symbols have kept their meanings to this day. Think of the valentine heart; it doesn't look much like the fist-sized organ that beats in our chest, but we instantly know it represents ardor. In my collection there are lots of hearts, as well as such love charms as flowers, lovers' knots, and Cupid's arrows. But I've also revived another

sentimental Victorian tradition: the spelling out of endearments with colored stones. My "dearest" egg pendant is encircled by faux versions of a diamond, an emerald, an amethyst, a ruby, another emerald, a sapphire, and a topaz. This is no random grouping; if you look at the first letter of the name of each stone, you'll see that together they spell out dearest. Sweet, yes? The woman who wears that luscious little egg knows that it's more than a pretty piece of jewelry. She knows it bears a secret message, meant just for her, and she wears it close to her heart.

SWEET INSPIRATION

Long before the sun rose and set on the British Empire, jewelry was infused with a powerful magic. In ancient times, colored stones were thought to heal and protect; earrings and necklaces indicated tribal status; sacred amulets warded off evil spirits.

When we read about it in anthropology books, the mystical qualities assigned to jewelry may seem pretty primitive. But think of jewelry's significance today: isn't the wedding band a powerful symbol of love and commitment? Maybe you've worn a class ring, or a gold cross, or a Star of David; maybe you've earned a gold watch, or even a Purple Heart.

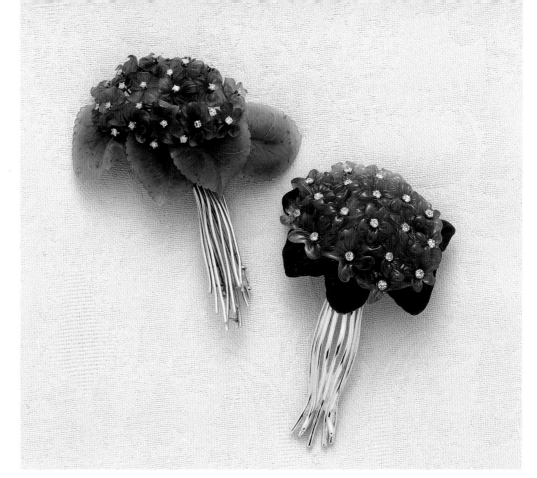

This exquisite bouquet of violets was once worn by a Victorian lady on her winter furs. Its amethyst petals are set with diamonds, and its jade leaves grow out of a fragile forest of gold stems. The Classics Collection version on the right is just as endearing. Like the original, it speaks of the eternal promise of spring, of tiny violets peeking through the snow.

The Queen of England would be nowhere without her crown; visitors to the Vatican line up to kiss the Pope's ring; and Miss America's greatest moment involves a glittery, tilted tiara. I could name a dozen more good examples of jewelry-as-totem (silver anniversaries, diamond jubilees, birthstones), but the point is this: jewelry today is every bit as symbolic as it was in ancient Egypt.

Not every piece of jewelry carried grand cultural significance, of course. But most of us own something that means a lot to us on a personal level. Myself, I'm inspired by the symbol of the bee, so much so that I've adopted it as the logo — the mascot, as it were — for the entire Joan Rivers Classics Collection. I relate to the bee because it accomplishes  the impossible every day. In aerodynamic terms, you understand, bees shouldn't be able to fly at all. Their bodies are too heavy, their wings are too small. Yet there they go, flying in the face of science, humming their tunes and pollinating like mad.

At a particularly daunting time of my life, Edgar gave me a bee brooch to remind me that anything is possible, as long as one's will is strong and one's spirit is intact. I took that message to heart, and that little bee has seen me through wonderful times and horrible times. In turn I've produced bracelets, brooches, and watches that honor the bee and its message of hope. And did I tell you that my daughter's name, Melissa, means "bee" in Greek? It's pure inspiration, that bee, and its form is utterly beautiful to me.

Another of my favorite symbols is the turtle. It reminds me of Aesop's fable about the tortoise and the hare, the one in which the slow and steady tortoise wins the race. It also calls to mind a phrase I once read: "Behold the turtle! He makes progress only when he sticks his neck out." Every time I touch my golden turtle pin I'm encouraged to carry on, to keep sticking my neck out.

Yes, jewelry is powerful. It can represent your roots, your beliefs, your philosophies. It can ground you and remain constant as the northern star, even when all of life is in flux — which in itself is a kind of magic.

ROMANCING THE STONE

Remember the adventures of Lorelei Lee in *Gentlemen Prefer Blondes?* She was that ditzy show girl whose every waking moment was dedicated to getting men to buy her diamonds. Of course, gifts of jewels are usually given with far more sentiment — and received rather more graciously — than the ones that ended up on Lorelei's fingers, wrists, neck, and ears. Still, there is a space between lovers that has always, it seems, been linked by gems and precious metals. The everlasting beauty of jewelry draws us in, fuels passions, and makes a love-gift for all time.

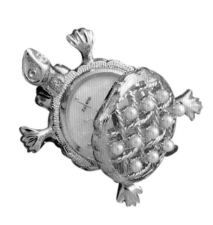

One very romantic piece in my personal collection is a brooch given by Edward VII to his mistress, Mrs. Keppel. It's an enormous red tourmaline encircled by a diamond snake. Though the brooch is extraordinarily opulent (Lorelei would have *loved* it), its symbolism is

This brooch is where romance and history converge. The original (on the left) was presented by King Edward VII to his famous mistress, Mrs. Keppel. It's centered around a rare red tourmaline; the snake of eternal love, rendered in platinum set with diamonds, encircles it protectively. I gave ours a slightly more modern look by enlarging the stones and setting it in gold, but its sinuous curves carry the same symbolism and the same juicy story as the original. P.S.: Rumor has it that even after she got the brooch, Mrs. Keppel still had to curtsy before getting into bed with the king.

what makes it special. Think of it: a rare, fiery gem (Mrs. Keppel, I presume) is embraced by a snake wrapped around itself — a symbol of eternal love — yet the snake's head is facing outward in a protective posture. Such passion!

And speaking of passion . . . don't believe for a second that jewelry itself isn't a form of flirtation. Sparkling ears, dazzling fingers, a fascinating glint at the throat; all these speak of a woman's spirit, the fire inside. When a woman wears jewelry she feels fascinating and provocative. And if she feels sexy, she's not only going to look sexy, she's going to *be* sexy. Which is just another reason why men love to give jewelry to women, and women love to get it.

IF IT FEELS GOOD, WEAR IT

Jewelry is many things to many people. But amid all the talk of romance, symbolism, historical significance, versatility, and practicality, let's not forget that jewelry is ultimately fun. Thank God for all the silly, frivolous things in life! Every once in a while I come across a piece of jewelry that absolutely delights me, that releases my imagination and puts a smile on my face.

Fabergé created this four-strand pearl choker at the turn of the century and crowned it with a detachable clasp of diamonds, dominated by a large black diamond. Our version, on the right, also has a clasp that detaches to become a pin, and the necklace can be worn with the clasp at the nape of the neck for a more simple, uncluttered look.

My teddy bear pin, for instance, turns me into an immature twelve-year-old. I perch him by the bed, play exorcist by turning his head 180 degrees, waggle his little arms, kiss his face. I love the fluttering wings on my moth pin, too, and the colorful flower pin that spins like a pinwheel. I could amuse myself for hours among interchangeable pendants, magnetized stones on rings, brooches that separate to become earrings, and pins that open to reveal watches.

Of course, many of these pieces are elegant as well as playful. Think of the pendant that can leave an impression in sealing wax, or the lorgnette that magnifies anything you point it at, or the necklace that ties like a lariat. By donning jewels like these a woman can be witty without having to say a word. What a gift to oneself!

When all is said and done, jewelry *is* a marvelous gift to oneself, a special, private delight. Whether we choose a simple gold chain or an elaborate crystal pin, jewelry reminds us of what it means to be female. It doesn't matter if we're all dolled up in a little black dress or running to the market in blue jeans and a sweatshirt; each of us is complex, multi-faceted, and precious. And we can celebrate ourselves and express our inner beauty with small treasures that are, in themselves, beautiful.

"Cartier is the Tiffany of jewelry stores." — Joan Rivers, *Enter Talking*

No jewel is an island. Like all decorative arts, jewelry design is part of an ongoing evolution of style; designers borrow from the past, take what's old and make it new again. You may think that your favorite chain-link necklace is an original, but it's probably a distant relative of one made by Bulgari. The glittering clasp on your triple-strand pearls was likely inspired by the great Fabergé; even your diamond ring may shine more brightly because of a Tiffany setting. Within my collection are echoes of Cartier (Art Deco), Van Cleef & Arpels (no-holds-barred opulence), Harry Winston (fabulous stones), and Verdura (imagination unlimited). Though the story of jewelry is as old as

Tiffany. From top to bottom: 18-karat gold compact; 18-karat gold table clock; pink sapphire and demantoid garnet fish brooch; gold and diamond flower brooch. All designed by Jean Schlumberger.

the story of humankind, we begin our overview of modern design with the year 1837, and follow the passionate careers of those visionaries who have defined beauty in our time.

Tiffany & Co.

Tiffany's! The name itself is magic. It's Audrey Hepburn in an evening gown, eating Danish and waiting for her future at the corner of 57th Street and Fifth Avenue. It's the destination of movie stars, lovers, and tycoons; it's "Moon River and me," a place where fantasy and reality converge. Tiffany's is so much a part of the American dream that even its signature box — the pale blue promise, the white ribbon of hope — is a treasure in itself. No one ever throws a Tiffany's box away. It's not a container; it's a trophy.

Though Tiffany & Co.'s mystique is eternal, its history is somewhat convoluted. It all began in 1837, when Charles Tiffany and John Young opened a "curiosity shop" on lower Broadway, stocked with inexpensive knickknacks and baubles imported from Europe. As the shop grew, the partners launched first into the sale and then into the manufacturing of fine gold jewelry. While such merchandising was highly successful — the company continually moved into ever-larger quarters — the Tiffany legend as we know it really began with diamonds. Because of political unrest in Europe in 1848, Young was able to go overseas and purchase extravagant jewels, including a great number of high-quality diamonds, from royal estates. Back in New York, the partners had the brilliant idea of putting the treasures on display in a "diamond parlor," thus forging a marriage between diamonds and Tiffany's that has lasted to this day.

The firm's reputation was sealed in 1853, when Charles Tiffany took over the helm. Charles had a genius for self-promotion, and he worked to keep the Tiffany name in the public eye. In 1870 he commissioned the city's first fireproof building; there he established an "Art Emporium," a museumlike display of bronze statuary, clocks, lamps, porcelain, and glassware. "Seeing Tiffany's in an afternoon," said one observer, "is like seeing Europe in three months."

Tiffany took his show on the road, too. At a time when most Americans had never seen a real diamond, Tiffany's spectacular jewelry displays caused a sensation at national exhibitions. At the 1876 Philadelphia Centennial, for instance, Tiffany & Co. showed a hair ornament in the shape of a peacock feather. At its center was a thirty-carat diamond surrounded by more than six hundred smaller diamonds, forming "quills" that fluttered at the lightest touch. Imagine the impact that feather must have had on glamour-starved America!

When Charles Tiffany died in 1902 an era of showmanship ended and a new, design-driven spirit was born. While famed Tiffany artisans such as Edward C. Moore and Paulding Farnham continued to create elaborate jewels made from rare and unusual gemstones, Tiffany's son, Louis Comfort Tiffany, founded the "Art Jewelry" department. Louis was an accomplished Impressionist painter who transferred the colors of his canvases into luminous ornaments made of gold, enamel, and colored stones. His creations had a free-form, handmade appearance that set them apart from the mainstream; though he's best remembered for his fabulous stained-glass lamps and windows, one of Louis's accomplishments was that he paved the way for individual artistic expression within the house of Tiffany.

The store moved to its present location in 1940 and subsequently became the address of some of the finest jewelry designers of the century. To me, the most memorable was Jean Schlumberger, who sought to create pieces that looked, in his words, as if they were "growing, uneven, at random, organic, in motion." His masterpieces were marked by an exquisite attention to detail and a masterful use of such techniques as enameling. Schlumberger was the first of Tiffany's "signature" designers; in later years, Elsa Peretti and Paloma Picasso joined that select group.

Today there is much at Tiffany's to love, from stationery items to poetic statements in precious gems. Still, it is the Tiffany mystique that is most alluring. The famous box, the rooms full of impossible treasures waiting to be coveted — this is what continues to draw dreamers to that mythical corner of 57th and Fifth.

FABERGÉ

It's no secret: I absolutely adore Fabergé jewels. When I close my eyes and think about all that Fabergé means to me, I see luxury in the extreme, perfect stones set in graceful frames, an embarrassment of ornament ordered into symmetry by brilliantly executed design. And I never forget that, amid all the legendary opulence, many of Fabergé's jewels display a great wit and a wonderful sense of playfulness. His work delighted the imperial Russian courts in those dramatic years between 1884 and 1918, and his creations continue to thrill us today.

When I say "Fabergé," of course, I'm referring to Peter Carl Fabergé. He's the man who, at the age of only twenty-four, took over his father's modest jewelry shop in St. Petersburg and turned it into perhaps the most influential design house of all time. At its height, the Fabergé empire employed nearly five hundred artisans and was in production seven days a week. All that energy, industry, and influence was poured into a single idea, which in its day was considered revolutionary: that the value of an object was to be found in its design and craftsmanship, and not necessarily in the combined value of its materials.

Up until young Fabergé burst on the scene, the overriding philosophy among Russian jewelers had been "more is more." That is, they had worked to cram as many large stones as possible into showy, often ill-conceived pieces. Carl, as he was known, chose to concentrate on details. He would study the exact shade of a Siberian emerald, or the cut of a fragment of Baltic amber, or the luminescence of a Russian aquamarine, and would then seek a perfect complementary setting. As a result each necklace, brooch, and tiara produced by the house of Fabergé was a unique composition, a complete work of art unto itself.

Of course, we best remember Fabergé for his fabulous eggs, the

first of which was presented by Czar Alexander III to Czarina Maria in 1884. The eggs became an immediate favorite of the court, and the traditional Easter gift among Russian royalty. It is estimated that a grand total of fifty-eight Fabergé eggs were produced, each more dazzling than the last. Some eggs were entirely decorative, objects of beauty to touch and hold; others contained "surprises," opening to reveal such treasures as a miniature basket of spring flowers rendered in semiprecious stones, or a tiny bird designed to sing on the hour, or even a minuscule replica of a train, the Trans-Siberian Express, which could be removed from the egg, wound with a key, and made to run.

Sadly, the extraordinary output of the house of Fabergé came to a dramatic end during the first bloody days of the Russian Revolution in 1917. Though Peter Carl Fabergé died in exile in Switzerland in 1920, his work lives on. In a span of only thirty-five years, his design house set worldwide standards of artistry. Carl's vision, so strong and sure in its day, seems even clearer now. As any connoisseur, curator, or collector will tell you, the pricelessness of all things Fabergé is based not on precious materials but on a masterful craftsmanship that has remained unrivaled for a hundred years.

Fabergé. My star sapphire and diamond brooch.

CARTIER

Throughout history, many of the great jewelry houses were just that — groups of designers who created wonderful jewelry. But the house of Cartier was something different: it was a house of *style*. In its heyday, which was about 1900 to 1940, the Cartier brothers served as tastemakers to the world. They produced not only jewelry but clocks, watches, cases, desk sets, compacts, handbags, lamps, picture frames . . . the list goes on and on. Each piece, in addition to being brilliantly crafted, was on the cutting edge of fashion and incorporated influences from such far-flung sources as Versailles, royal India, untamed Africa, ancient Egypt, and the Ballets Russes.

Which brings us to the story of Louis, Pierre, and Jacques, the globe-trotting Cartier brothers who made it all happen. They had been born to an already-thriving jewelry business started by their grandfather, and had grown up under the tutelage of their father, Alfred Cartier. Alfred had successfully directed the family business to meet the needs of a growing European middle class, and had built up an international reputation based on excellent craftsmanship and traditional standards of good taste. In 1898, however, when Alfred's son Louis joined the firm, he and his brothers were ready, willing, and able to steer the business

Cartier. From top to bottom: citrine quartz and diamond flower brooch, earclips, clip, and brooch. All made in London, c. 1940.

into the new century. They promptly launched into a "divide and conquer" mode: Jacques opened a Cartier store in London; Pierre went overseas and established a branch in New York; Louis stayed on at the central workshop in Paris.

A pivotal moment in the history of Cartier took place in Paris in 1909: Louis witnessed a performance of the Ballets Russes. The brightly colored, wildly exotic sets and costumes employed by the troupe grabbed the young Cartier. He had seen the future of style and hired a twenty-four-year-old designer, Charles Jacqueau, to capture the thrilling new look. Jacqueau turned out to be the right man for the job. He not only electrified Cartier's jewelry designs but incorporated elements of Indian, Egyptian, Chinese, and Japanese design to develop a style that came to be known as Art Deco. A second Cartier coup came in the form of Jeanne Toussaint, who joined the Cartier team in 1910 at the age of twenty-three. She was a thoroughly modern woman who was able to understand and anticipate the needs of the increasingly liberated twentieth-century female. Her line of accessories, including handbags, makeup cases, and jewelry that complemented the sleek, body-hugging fashions of the day, became "must-haves" for a new generation of women. With Jacqueau and

Toussaint in the house, the Cartier name became synonymous with all that was fresh, exciting, and important; in comparison, "traditional" jewels seemed hopelessly old-fashioned, dusty relics of a bygone era.

The house of Cartier rode the crest of tastes and attitudes through decade after decade of worldwide turmoil and ever-changing styles. As early as 1915, the house produced the first of its famous panthers, which eventually became a Cartier signature. In the 1940s a new generation of Cartier sons and daughters began exerting their influence, and in 1973 *Le Must de Cartier* was launched. This mass-production venture put the Cartier name in boutiques all over the globe. Although *Le Must* was highly successful by marketing standards, the Cartier brothers had by then, alas, passed on, leaving their legacy but ending a half-century of extraordinary energy and unique vision.

VAN CLEEF & ARPELS

Remember those stories about Barbara Hutton, who, it was said, so loved her diamond tiara that she wore it to bed? And remember those old photos of Elizabeth Taylor prancing around in an outrageous tiara that framed her 1960s top knot? If so, then you already know the work of

Van Cleef & Arpels. The Parisian-based house has always, it seems, been *the* source of luxury and extravagance. They created wedding gifts for Princess Grace's marriage to Prince Rainier of Monaco in 1957. In the 1930s they bedecked the stylish bosom of the Duchess of Windsor. Their gems have been worn by generations of Vanderbilts, Mellons, and Kennedys; and for nearly a century, Van Cleef & Arpels treasures have been presented at royal courts all over the world. I'm not exaggerating; clients have included the Duke of Westminster, the Aga Khan, King Farouk, the Maharajah of Baroda, Queen Nazli of Egypt, the Prince of Nepal, the Shah of Iran . . . Shall I go on?

Of course, it wasn't *all* crowns and scepters for the partners. Their firm began in 1906 with a simple convergence of talents. Alfred Van Cleef came from a family of master lapidary craftsmen and was himself a skilled stonecutter, administrator, and strategist. Charles and Julien Arpels, brothers of Van Cleef's wife, Estelle, had similar backgrounds, plus the kind of charm and savoir faire that attracted influential members of Parisian society. The partners were joined in 1912 by another Arpels brother, Louis, and together they worked to create distinctive, high-end jewelry for a privileged and discriminating clientele.

Van Cleef & Arpels. From top to bottom: invisibly set sapphire and diamond flower brooch, bracelet (both made in New York), and pendant-earclips (made in Paris).

Within their grand vision the partners were always informed by contemporary movements. For example, in 1922, when "Tutmania" swept through Europe and America, the house of Van Cleef & Arpels introduced a line of jewelry that took the Sphinx, scarabs, and other Egyptian icons as its principal motifs. When Art Deco hit the scene, their designs came to life in eye-catching bracelets and bold earrings that complemented the flapper's penchant for bobbed hair and bare arms. They often created "convertible" jewelry, pieces that could be taken apart and worn in different ways; they made a huge splash in the 1930s with a series of jeweled boxes designed to be used as evening bags; and, in 1935 they developed the "invisible setting," which allowed fitted stones to be placed seamlessly against one another.

In the post-war years, when women were more likely to attend an office party than a coronation, Van Cleef & Arpels came through with lines of jewelry that were still luxurious, but less flashy and more practical. Perfect examples are those wonderful, snaky necklaces and bracelets made from rows of flat, gold hexagons that the ever-inventive house began producing in the 1940s. In the 1970s and 1980s, a new generation of Arpels designers made their mark with a series of "Ribbons" and "Bows," motifs that are still popular today.

As venerable as always, Van Cleef & Arpels is still in the hands of the Arpels family. Its shops are a staple of exclusive neighborhoods in Manhattan, Palm Beach, Beverly Hills, and Tokyo. And, if you're ever in Paris, stop in at 22, place Vendôme, the address where it all began nearly a hundred years ago, and where the Arpels family continues to produce jewelry suitable for royalty.

HARRY WINSTON

They called him the "king of diamonds." He was the man who steamed across oceans or flew across continents whenever a large, rare gem came up for auction or emerged from obscurity. He was consulted by heads of state, heiresses, collectors, and even other gemologists before an extraordinary stone was to be appraised, cut, or set. At one time or another he owned more than a third of the famous diamonds of the world — more than any king or emperor — and it seems as though, for Harry Winston, it was all easy destiny.

Harry Winston was born in New York in 1896. His earliest training in gemology came from his father, who owned a modest jewelry store, but even at a very young age Harry's instinct for gemstones was uncanny. He once commented that he must have been born with some knowledge of jewels; one sign of his innate ability occurred at the age of twelve, when he spotted a green-stoned ring in a pawnshop window. Young Harry bought the ring for twenty-five cents, then sold it two days later for eight hundred dollars. It was, as he'd suspected, a two-carat emerald. At age fifteen Harry began working at his family's shop in Los Angeles, but it wasn't long before he broke away, returned to New York, and opened the Premier Diamond Company on Fifth Avenue.

Harry's razzle-dazzle salesmanship and extraordinary eye for gems earned him a good reputation among New York's diamond merchants, but in 1922 an unscrupulous employee robbed him of his hard-won cash and jewels. Though his company was literally cleaned out, the disaster paved the way for Harry's brilliant future: it was then that he shifted his focus and began to buy estate jewelry. In those days the market was flooded with Victorian and Edwardian jewels that were sorely out of fashion. Harry's idea was to buy up these bargain-priced "relics," re-cut the stones for greater sparkle, then mount them in contemporary settings.

While accessing and purchasing estates, Harry began to amass a store of unusually large, high-quality gemstones. In 1932 he incorporated under his own, increasingly famous name; by 1949 his collection of rare gems was so vast that he assembled a touring exhibition called the "Court of Jewels." The exhibit included the 46-carat Hope diamond, the 95-carat Star of the East, the 126-carat Jonker diamond, the 337-carat Catherine the Great sapphire, and the famous Inquisition necklace, whose stones date back to Spanish plunder of the Incas.

Harry Winston made a fortune in the jewelry trade. But his lifetime of fabulous acquisitions had, in his mind, much more to do with beauty than with money. He genuinely loved precious stones, so much so that he was known to keep one in his jacket pocket just to fondle. (At one time his touchstone was the 76-carat Star of Independence, which sold in 1977 for $4 million.) His wife, Edna, who often accompanied him on his worldwide buying adventures, referred to diamonds as Harry's "babies." After a particularly large sale, she recalled, he'd often go through a period of mourning.

It's no surprise that the house of Winston became known for designs that highlighted the luminosity of great jewels. The Winston signature style, originally inspired by a wreath of holly, employed wires of platinum and gold. These "independent prong settings" were nearly invisible and

Harry Winston.
My diamond flower brooch
with removable "stem."

wonderfully fluid; Harry bragged that his bracelets could be "crumpled like a sweater," yet not one stone would touch the other. Another Winston hallmark was the framing of large, colored stones with smaller diamonds, as if the central stone were a luminous painting.

Harry Winston died in 1978, but his name will always be linked with the great stones of the world. The Taylor-Burton, the Mabel Boll, the Louis XIV, the Liberator, the Star of Sierra Leone, and many other famous diamonds were cut to flawless perfection by the house of Harry Winston. Perhaps even more precious are the stones — the Hope, the 127-carat Portuguese, and the 254-carat Oppenheimer — that Harry donated to the Smithsonian Institution as gifts to the American people.

Verdura

The story of Verdura is a charmed tale of riches to riches. It started with a birth: the year was 1898, the place was Palermo, Sicily, and the baby who came into the world was Fulco Santostefano della Cerda, Duke of Verdura and Marquess of Murata la Cerda. Mind you, dukes are not generally destined to become jewelry designers. But Verdura was born into an eccentric family who indulged his every whim and surrounded him with

Verdura. From top to bottom: black onyx jeweled "Byzantine" bangle bracelet; black onyx jeweled "Maltese cross" bangle bracelet; 18-karat gold and scallop shell brooch; amethyst and diamond ring; black onyx and colored stone earclips.

books, gardens, and exotic animals — all of which contributed to his budding artistic talent and to an imagination that would eventually become legendary.

When Verdura came of age, he set off to taste the high life in Cannes, Venice, and Paris. In 1926 he had the good fortune to meet Linda and Cole Porter, who encouraged him to develop his visual talents; he took their advice and dispatched himself to Paris. There, he went to work for none other than Coco Chanel. Coco immediately recognized that, besides excellent breeding, the young man had talent; she-of-unerring-taste asked the fledgling designer to update her line of jewelry. Among other masterpieces, Verdura proceeded to create two items that, even today, serve as signature pieces for the house of Chanel. One was a pair of wide cuff bracelets, enameled and encrusted with a dazzling Maltese cross. The other was a simple yet dramatic pair of earrings featuring large pearls surrounded by gold braid, a design that is still imitated everywhere.

Verdura could have been satisfied with his European triumphs. Instead, with brilliant social contacts in his pocket and outrageous ideas in his head, he came to the United States to seek his second fortune. He began by designing jewelry for Paul Flato in New York. When Flato opened a store in Los Angeles, Verdura was asked to run it, and thus began a Hollywood romance. This was 1937, you understand, when Tinseltown was dripping in diamonds, and movie stars were ready for Verdura's innovations. Major celebrities, including Marlene Dietrich, Rita Hayworth, Gary Cooper, and Katharine Hepburn, clamored not only for Verdura's designs but also for his friendship. Though he rapidly became a legend among legends, Verdura opted to return to New York. There, in 1939, he opened his own shop on Fifth Avenue with financial backing from his old friend Cole Porter.

Verdura's jewels were an immediate success. He had a lush, sensual touch that played itself out in images from nature, including animals, fruits, flowers, and undersea creatures. He was the first to incorporate organic elements into his work, and often built opulent pieces of jewelry around actual shells collected from the beach. He shunned large diamonds and imposing stones, calling them "mineralogy, not jewelry," and preferred to utilize simpler materials to execute innovative motifs such as ropes, leaves, garlands, and ribbons. Color, too, was important to Verdura; one of his signature pieces was a leaf-shaped brooch executed in sapphires and zircons that ranged in color from golden yellow to rich brown.

Verdura died in 1978. But when you look at contemporary jewelry by Paloma Picasso, Elsa Peretti, and dozens of other designers, you can see the Verdura legacy; his motives were always genuine, and his influence was born of an art that came not from need but from desire, a true passion that continues to resonate.

BULGARI

As far as I'm concerned, the house of Bulgari *invented* the "Italian look." Heavy gold chains surrounding large, luminous cabochons . . . stones that carry the intense colors of the Mediterranean . . . a rich Renaissance aesthetic brought to life in precious jewels — these would not be ours if it weren't for the Bulgari brothers.

Giorgio and Costantino Bulgari, the two brothers who founded the jewelry empire, started out as engravers. They were taught the trade by their Greek-born father, Sotirio, a silversmith who operated a small shop in Rome. They took over the business in the 1920s, eventually switching their focus from engraving to the production of jewelry, and in the 1930s opened a store at 10 via Condotti.

As the business grew, Giorgio and Costantino immersed themselves

*Bulgari and
Harry Winston.
From top to bottom:
diamond earrings,
mounted by Harry
Winston; diamond
and sapphire earclips,
Bulgari; 18-karat gold
and diamond necklace,
Bulgari; diamond
earclips, Bulgari.*

in both the history of Italian art and the modern jewelry-making techniques of Paris. At the time, jewelry design was dominated by the "French style," built on the basic configuration of a faceted diamond set in prongs and surrounded by emeralds, rubies, or sapphires. While the public's taste in jewelry was beginning to broaden, thanks to an exposure to motifs from the Middle East, India, Egypt, and other "exotic" locales, it was up to the Bulgaris to initiate a revival of the forms and colors of the Italian Renaissance.

And they did it with a vengeance. The brothers revived the use of brightly colored stones cut in the cabochon style (polished to a clear, smooth dome, without facets). For many of their designs they set a centerpiece stone in a smooth gold bezel, framed it with tapered baguette diamonds, then encased the whole arrangement in a heavy gold chain. They often used contrasting materials to form strong, geometric patterns — a stripe of diamonds would play against a stripe of solid gold, for instance, supporting a central chevron of rubies. Their work was less about images and motifs than about form and pattern. Like the aesthetic that ruled ancient Rome and was later embraced by Renaissance artists, the Bulgari spirit was Classical rather than Romantic.

A scholarly interest in history led the Bulgari boys to create an entire vocabulary of styles that we take for granted today. They were the first to turn handmade gold chains into fine jewelry, and the first to integrate antique coins into jewelry designs. They revived the use of yellow gold (up until then, platinum and white gold were the preferred materials) and reintroduced both cameo and intaglio techniques into the mainstream. Perhaps most important, the Bulgaris brought a whole new sense of color to the international jewelry scene. The colors of emeralds, rubies, and sapphires had long ruled the palette of jewelry; the house of Bulgari utilized new combinations of colors, such as pinks, violets, and yellows.

It's hard to believe that all these innovations happened in the second part of this century. Think of it: the first Bulgari shop outside of Rome was opened in New York in 1970. From there, under the management of Giorgio's three sons, Bulgari expanded to Geneva, Monte Carlo, and Paris in the 1970s, then Milan, Tokyo, Hong Kong, Osaka, Singapore, London, and Munich in the 1980s. In the 1990s the house of Bulgari continues to thrive; from its workshops in Rome we inherit the entire magnificent history of Italy, all wrapped in a luminous package of wearable art.

The Wand and the Wardrobe

Have you ever sat down and made a list of all the roles that you, as a woman, fulfill in day-to-day life? You should try it sometime. You may end up with pages and pages of titles, including — just for starters — mother, wife, friend, girlfriend, businesswoman, daughter, boss, sister, chef, maid, chauffeur, athlete, hostess, shopper, baby-sitter, in-law, correspondent, traveler, psychologist, matinee lady, and nurse. Now, imagine that you had a different outfit for every role you played. Impossible, right? You'd need ten walk-in closets just to get through the week. These days, our lives are so hectic and so diverse that the average woman has to be a kind of fashion sorceress. From a modest closet

If you're seeking a look that commands respect yet is decidedly feminine, try gold, white, and black jewels against a simple black suit. With this ensemble by Chanel I'm wearing gold and black button earrings with crystal details; a black enamel and ivory Maltese cross brooch; a long gold chain and matching bracelet studded with pearls and jet-black beads; a necklace bearing a black intaglio pendant; a gold-toned bracelet watch; plus two coordinating rings and two coordinating bracelets. When you add it all up it's a lot of jewelry, but when you put it all together it makes an outfit that's amazingly uncluttered.

of basics she must conjure outfits that are comfortable, stylish, flattering, and appropriate in any number of situations. What's more, she's got to feel right about what she puts on in the morning — she's got to feel that she's putting her best self forward and that her outfit is helping her enjoy every minute of every day. It's quite an accomplishment. Luckily, it can be made much easier and much more fun with the help of jewelry.

With the drop of an earring, a woman can transform the look and feel of a single outfit. Think, for example, of an easy sweep of black jersey — a calf-length dress, say. Add hoop earrings, an armload of bangles, and a fun, jingling necklace, and you're ready for a day of shopping and a bite of Mexican food. Now try that very same dress with cascades of pearls. Voilà! Your table is ready, your champagne is chilled. You say you have a big day at the office, then a PTA meeting? How about a single long pendant and a pair of coordinating clips? For luncheon with Aunt Alice, wear the dress with a gold link necklace and a pair of cuffs; or, at holiday time, transform it into party clothes by adding a glittering assortment of colored gemstones. See? One simple dress becomes five entirely different outfits. Women really *are* sorceresses, and jewelry is our magic wand.

IN PRAISE OF EARRINGS

Never underestimate the power of earrings — they are the jewels that dress your face. Earrings can accentuate the line of your neck or make your cheekbones stand out; they can draw attention to your hairstyle, your jawline, even your smile. Perhaps most important, earrings reflect the beauty of your eyes. Look at yourself in the mirror: first you'll notice the sparkle and glow of your own eyes, those God-given jewels in which so much can be seen. Second, just beyond and slightly lower, you'll catch a second set of twinkling gems. When you think of it, earrings not only frame the face but really are like another pair of beautiful eyes. Like our eyes, they speak volumes about who we are. Unlike our eyes, we can change them as often as we want.

When buying earrings, take a good look at your face, hairstyle, and neckline. If your features are small or your bone structure is delicate, you'll probably look best in petite button earrings, studs, or drops. Conversely, if your features are strong or your bone structure is pronounced, larger, splashier earrings will probably flatter you best. Hairstyles are important to consider, too: short, chic 'dos are a natural showcase for earrings and look great with everything from twinkling studs to shiny showstoppers. Longer,

It's comfortable, it's casual, it's stylish. A classic sweater — this one is part of a set from Barney's New York — is always correct for the office or for easy entertaining at home, but it's made even better with the right accessories. Cluster earrings, featuring Tahitianlike pearls with crystal accents, pick up the luminescence of a double strand of Tahitian-style pearls. A daytime watch keeps stylish time; a link bracelet falls deliciously about the wrist; and the fun of the ring on that extended hand is that its stone is held on by a magnet — because everyone knows that it's a woman's prerogative to change her mind.

fuller hairstyles are more of a challenge; they call for earrings that stand out from the face yet don't get lost in the length.

Now examine your neckline: is it long and swanlike or shorter and more athletic-looking? While women with very long necks can wear almost any style with ease, shorter-necked women should avoid extremely long earrings that "connect" the space between the ear and the shoulder. In any case, no earring should "crash" against the collarbone — that's just *too* long!

Besides choosing the right shapes and styles for your face, there are some great little tricks that can be played with earrings. For instance, no matter what color your eyes may be, they will be ultra-enhanced by earrings that match. Want to downplay a less-favorite facial feature? Long, dangling earrings tend to slenderize the face because they accentuate length rather than width. A less-than-firm jawline will tighten right up with the addition of large, strong clips, especially if they're geometrically shaped. And how about those earlobes? One of Mother Nature's less charming gifts is that, as we age, our earlobes tend to become elongated. Button-style earrings are a brilliant way to disguise that problem, and many earrings combine both buttons and drops — so your options are almost unlimited.

While we should always wear what pleases us, there are, in the land of earrings, certain combinations that almost always work. For a fun, casual look, try slim hoop earrings with a velvet baseball cap or woolen beret. Sporty outfits — even tennis whites or ski gear — look great with simple little studs. On special occasions, fancy up-'dos practically beg for big, dramatic earrings that glitter by candlelight; if you're into back-swept hairstyles, such as French braids or ponytails, try some short drop earrings.

Finally, consider where you will be when you're seen in your earrings. If you're, say, giving a presentation at the lawn club or accepting an award for best actress, you may be tempted to wear those tiny diamonds — but who will know except you and a few sharpies in the first row? When you're going to be seen from a distance, go for drama. Conversely, intimate situations call for intimate jewelry. I could make an argument for wearing little stud earrings with your nightgown, even if your "nightgown" is a football jersey. Why not? Earrings, among their other powers, can make us feel feminine and flirty in almost any situation.

NECKLACES, NAUGHTY AND NICE

There was a wonderful fashion moment in the beginning of the seventeenth century when stylish French ladies started doing something shocking: they began going around in public without their collars. Which means, of course, that their shoulders and upper chests were on flagrant display. Which is how we inherited the word *décolletage* (literally, "uncollaring"). Which paved the way for the Golden Age of Necklaces. Which, as far as I'm concerned, is now.

What fun it is to decorate ourselves, to drape our shoulders with pretty beads and shining strands! Think of elegant chokers and sparkling pendants, sentimental lockets and interlocking links; imagine elaborate lorgnettes on long golden chains, charm necklaces that jingle and swing. Even though the inspiration for many of today's designs dates back hundreds of years, there's something about a necklace that never looks dated.

One of the great advantages of necklaces is their flexibility. You can wear necklaces on their own or drape them in multiples. You can take a single gold chain and hang it with a pendant or a locket; that same gold chain can become a jingling circle of baubles with the addition of some favorite charms. Have you tried a string of pearls worn together with a string of jet beads? How about three different chains dangling three different pendants? You're limited only by your imagination.

When starting your own collection of necklaces, keep in mind that

Maybe you're headed for a luncheon with friends, or maybe you've invited Mr. Wonderful for an intimate dinner at home. Earth tones are a good choice — they're always warm and inviting, as you can see by this three-piece Pamela Dennis ensemble — and my version of Queen Marie of Romania's necklace is the perfect complement. Certain jewels are intimate by nature. They want to be touched, twirled in the hand, or, in the case of this necklace, read like chapters in an ever-unfolding story. With so much visual dialogue in a single necklace, one barely needs anything else. Just a touch of gold on the wrist and a bit of interest around the face are enough to make this a total ensemble.

necklace success begins with length. Your best necklace lengths depend on two factors: body type and the neckline of a particular outfit. Very long necklaces are best worn by smaller-chested women, because the necklaces themselves are most attractive when they're allowed to hang in a fluid, unbroken line. When a buxom woman wears a long necklace, that necklace will try to find "lower ground"— that is, it will work its way over to one side of her breasts, or will bounce around between them and start turning over on itself. So, if you've been blessed with a chest, your ideal choices may be choker-length necklaces or pendants that fall right above the bustline.

Certain clothes create the perfect showcase for necklaces, including off-the-shoulder styles, low scoop necks, V-necks, turtlenecks, and low, open collars. Shirts and blouses with crew necks or button-up collars are a little trickier; with these, you'll want to make sure that the necklace you choose doesn't cause the fabric to bunch up or "crawl." Also, look at the button on that blouse. Is it a perfect little jewel unto itself, or is it just plain boring? If it's dull, you may want to cover it with a coordinating pin, or choose a necklace style that obscures the button, that is, multiple-strand links.

PIN ME

A funny thing happened on the way to creating the Classics Collection: I was told that women didn't buy pins. Not that I cared about others' opinions, mind you. I've always come out with designs that I liked, ignoring curmudgeons and naysayers. But I must tell you that in this case the "industry experts" were wrong. Women love pins, buy pins, and wear pins. And that makes me happy, because I love, buy, and wear pins, too. I *always* wear a brooch with a blazer or suit jacket. Want to know why? Because a navy blazer is just a navy blazer, unless it carries a personal signature. That's what pins and brooches are; they come right out and say, "I am me, and no one else." You can't expect someone to remember that you wore a blazer, after all, but they'll definitely remember that shimmering Maltese cross you wore on the lapel.

A delightful way to wear pins is to group them together. This is best done with smaller "scatter" pins that have a common theme. A miniature menagerie of animal pins can be fun, and so can a sparkling collection of rhinestone pins or a spray of golden pins with colored stones.

Now, where to place that group of pins, or that favorite brooch? Here are some suggestions: (1) On the lapel of your winter coat. (2) On

For those occasions when you must look at once smashing and reserved, conservative yet imaginative, something along these lines would probably serve you well. The Renaissance-inspired suit, by Ralph Lauren, features a white ruff at the throat and a flutter of ruffles at the wrist, yet even an outfit this flamboyant benefits from an intelligent use of jewelry. The emerald brooch looks like it was born on that jacket, while two very different bracelets extend the lines of the suit and make the whole ensemble seem more personal. Earrings are a must, both to balance the look and to bring attention back to the face.

a denim jacket. (3) On a scarf, to hold it in place and/or to add interest. (4) On a beret, off to the side, just above the ear. (5) On a wide-brimmed hat, front and center. (6) On a solid-colored dress, in tandem, one pin placed higher than the other. (7) At a neckline, obscuring the uppermost button of a blouse. (8) On a blazer or suit jacket, either on the lapel or at a point between the shoulder and the bustline. (9) On a vest — perhaps a vest that's reserved especially for your favorite pins.

No matter what your choice, whether you're wearing a collection of scatter pins or showcasing one important piece, pins and brooches are a big voice in the fashion wilderness. Women not wear pins? Bah! We know better.

THE BRACELET'S EMBRACE

In terms of expressiveness, I believe that hands are second only to the face. Our hands have a language all their own; they can underscore ideas or make statements that escape words. Hands are a direct line to our subconscious. How many of us clap our hands in delight, sketch pictures in the air, or dismiss situations with a queenly gesture? While we're talking, working, or playing, our hands are performing a graceful ballet that, whether we know it or not, is both enlightening and enchanting. And all of this subliminal action is orbited by that beautiful shining circle we call the bracelet.

To me, there is something unfinished about an outfit that doesn't include a bracelet. Like the period at the end of a sentence, a bracelet announces, "This is where the cloth ends and the flesh begins. Feast your eyes!" And *what* a feast. Virtually every woman can wear bracelets with wild abandon, because bracelets don't care about age, weight, body type, or

Can we ever have enough glamour in our lives? This gown by Geoffrey Beene could win an Academy Award for sheer impact — but not without sparkling jewels in the supporting roles. Here, the "platinum look" is carried through with my Austrian crystal cuffs and glittering rings. Ah, glamour, life's dessert!

bone structure. They're always going to look fabulous, and they're always going to feel great. Don't you love the way a little grouping of bangles sings and jingles as you move? How about the sexy, snaky slip of a chain bracelet? Few things are more appealing than the sight of a woman reaching out and touching something (or someone) while a gentle choir of charms tinkles on her wrist.

In the summertime, when arms are tanned and sleeves are short, we reach for bracelets naturally, as a kind of fashion reflex. We pile them on both wrists; we wear matching cuffs as if to imply that our very skin is a sleeve. But bracelets are gorgeous in the winter, fall, and spring, too. They can jazz up an otherwise sober business suit or draw attention to a particularly attractive sleeve on a blouse. A plain jersey or sweater is instantly special when a sleeve is pushed up and a bracelet is revealed. Bracelets can be grouped in unusual ways to tell a kind of color story, or to play up contrasts between gold, silver, and jet black; and when night falls, a sparkling band around the wrist is a riveting detail. It becomes the center of rapt attention as we hold a fork, make a gesture, or reach, ever so gracefully, to tuck a stray tendril behind the ear. And that's why I never forget to decorate my wrists.

WATCH WORDS

We've been hearing all our lives that clothes make the man; with women, however, it's what one *does* with clothes that matters. Consider the watch. For most men, the watch is a utilitarian object. It keeps accurate time while resisting water and shock. It may also light up at night, beep on demand, go deep-sea diving, withstand extreme temperatures, and be an outrageously expensive status symbol. For most women, though, a watch has only two jobs: to keep time and look beautiful. And not necessarily in that order.

Remember your mother's "good watch"? Chances are it was a whisper of a thing studded with tiny, faceted gems and had a face no bigger than the stone on a cocktail ring. Women have long recognized that watches are jewelry-with-a-purpose — and really, if you're going to have to look at something once or twice an hour, why not look at something beautiful? Every well-dressed woman should have a few tailored (but feminine) watches for daytime, and at least one very dressy watch for evening. The elegant bracelet watch is always correct, day or night, but don't forget the less conventional options: there's something extraspecial about a sparkling brooch that hides a tiny timepiece, and, dangling languidly from a long chain, a fine watch is as luxurious as any pendant.

RING IN THE NEW

Those small shining circles, fitted just for us . . . what is more intimate
than the ring? We feel so much with our fingers — they are literally our
centers of touch. And yet rings, once in place, seem to become a part of
our bodies, constant companions that we wear like a second skin.

For many of us, the objects we most cherish in this world are our
rings, especially our engagement ring and our wedding ring. It's a
beautiful custom, the exchange of rings, and if you've ever wondered
where that tradition began, I can tell you right now: ancient Egypt. In
about 2800 B.C., wedding bands became part of the Egyptian marriage
ceremony; they were made of gold and signified, as do wedding bands
today, an eternal bond with no beginning and no end. Engagement rings
came along a few thousand years later, back when marriage was often a
kind of elaborate business transaction. The engagement ring signified
a pact not only between young men and women but between families of
wealth. For Roman Catholics, that tradition was sanctified by Pope
Nicholas I in 860 A.D., when he decreed that the engagement ring
become a required part of nuptial preparations. Was it taken seriously?
I'll say. Princess Mary, daughter of Henry VIII, was engaged at the

terrible age of two to the newborn dauphin of France — and don't you think she wore a tiny diamond engagement ring for all of Europe to see?

With so much tradition and symbolism attached to rings, it's no wonder that many of us slip into the comfortable habit of wearing the same rings, day in and day out. But let's not forget that a change of rings can make us feel brand new. The cocktail ring by its very name implies a splashy bauble of pure fantasy, meant to coordinate with whatever version of cocktail dresses the modern world may throw our way. Stack rings are loads of fun, too. With slim bands of glimmering crystals in different tones, a woman can pull together the colors of her outfit or simply make a bright and beautiful statement. And rings can maintain their symbolism even if they don't *look* traditional: I know a woman whose husband gave her a thin stack ring for each child they had together, done in the child's birthstone. She wore all three on one finger. What could be more beautiful and meaningful than that?

In the world of jewelry, rings are some of the only items that are sized. While most of us know the size of our "ring finger," let's not forget those nine other digits! A single dramatic stone on the forefinger is a great look (it's also where early Hebrews wore their wedding rings). Pinky rings are a great flash of fun because, more than any other finger, the pinky articulates the gestures of the hand. Even the thumb can be a site for a slim, shining band; it is, after all, the traditional "ring finger" in India. And speaking of ring fingers, did you know that our custom of placing wedding bands on the third finger of the left hand came from ancient Greece? Physicians in the third century B.C. believed that there was a "vein of love" running from that finger directly to the heart. Though their theory proved to be biologically untrue, the tradition has stayed with us, generation after generation. Perhaps it's because, in the language of love, there really is a direct line between our ring finger and our heart.

IT'S IN THE MIX

People often ask me about the "rules of fashion." It's a question that stumps me every time, because "rules of fashion" is really an oxymoron. Fashion is not now, nor has it ever been, a set of "dos" and "don'ts" carved on stone tablets in some secret cave. Fashion, like art or music, isn't a *thing* but a form of self-expression. It's a language without words, and to count its manifestations we'd have to count fingerprints, because each woman's style is strictly her own.

I'll never forget the moment when I saw and truly understood both the lawlessness and the impact of fashion. It was many years ago, in early spring, and I was one of about a dozen guests at a rather fancy dinner party. At my table was a woman wearing a pale pink suit made from a slightly nubby fabric. Her blouse was a cream-colored silk, high-necked; she wore her hair in a French twist; and around her neck were pearls. Wait, let me rephrase that: around her neck were *pearls*, miles of pearls, pearls draped in a dozen lengths that began close to her neck and descended all the way to her waist. Her pearls were a mix of weights and sizes, and various strands were punctuated with crystals, little hints of gold, and sparkling details that caught the light. At her ears were more pearls, lovely drops that moved with her, and on her wrists she wore two different kinds of pearl bracelets, plus a watch whose band was a triple strand of pearls. Does it all sound like too much? Yes, on paper it probably does. But in real life the look was astonishing, dazzling. I couldn't take my eyes off her — *nobody* could. It's not that this woman was young and gorgeous, you understand. But she was, in a word, magnificent. She outshone the candelabra, the place settings, the company, the food. Her presence added so much to the evening that she was kind of a

Architect Mies van der Rohe once stated that "less is more." Years later, designer Robert Venturi commented, "Less is a bore." I think I'll have to go with Venturi on that one. Though it's not for every occasion, this festival of crystals, blue stones, and fabulous faux pearls plays beautifully against a shimmering, silvery blouse by Gianfranco Ferré. As long as you stick to a central theme and choose pieces that complement one another, multiple jewels can create an unforgettable look that's packed with pizzazz.

centerpiece unto herself, and it seemed as though that party would have been nothing without her.

Now, that's only one side of my dinner-party story, because the Woman in Pearls did have competition, style-wise. And that competition came from a young woman at the other end of the table. She was wearing a simple, one-shouldered gown, and her long hair was brushed to one side, like Veronica Lake's, so that it curtained part of her face and curled against her bare shoulder. On her one exposed ear that woman wore a single spectacular earring, with more facets and colors than a stained-glass window at Notre Dame. It was the only piece of jewelry she wore. It was the only piece of jewelry she *needed*. Now, anybody who looked very closely could have seen that this young woman was no ravishing beauty. But who knew? Her style was so breathtaking and so complete that those little flaws — the slightly crooked nose, the too-high forehead — looked entirely intentional.

The moral of the story? Make your own style. Yes, you can mix gold and silver. Yes, you can pile on the jewels, lead the eye on a merry chase, make a game of hide-and-seek. Yes, go ahead, cluster pins, stack rings, and dangle bangles from both arms, or take it all off and wear a single, stunning piece. Yes, yes, a thousand times, yes.

W

hat started with a pearl necklace is now a wardrobe of bijoux, baubles, and jewels. Is there something for every-one in my collection? I don't know. But there is something for the tailored woman who likes to be audacious now and then. There's something for the woman who warms to the glint of gold, and for the woman who loves the glitter of crystal. There's powerful jewelry and jewelry that purrs, whimsical pieces and knock-out ensembles . . . A few of my favorites are cataloged on the following pages. Read on, and remember: though we say "pearl" and "ruby," the Joan Rivers Classics Collection features high-quality synthetic gems, faux pearls, and metals electroplated with 24-karat gold.

COLLECTOR'S ITEM
The Joan Rivers Classics Collection fifth-anniversary bracelet. Hinged cuff bracelet of gold, cabochon-cut rubies, pavé-set crystals, and emerald enamel; limited edition.

A WORLD OF PEARLS

Clockwise from upper left: *necklaces of Tahitian and white pearls; double strand of pearls with crystal rondelles and lariat-tie ends; seven-strand chain necklace with pearls; golden earrings with pearl drops; baroque pearl necklace with "lovers' knots"; baroque pearl necklace; seed pearl locket, shown as brooch; gold and pearl button earrings; Maltese cross pearl brooch; Tahitian pearl earrings with crystals; flower bracelet with seed pearls; bracelet of pearls and crystals; heart-shaped earrings with seed pearls, crystals, and garnets.*

THE PLEASURES OF PLATINUM

Overleaf: Left-hand page, clockwise from upper left: *pearl necklace with detachable crystal brooch inspired by Fabergé; platinum button earrings with pavé-set crystals; crystal bow earrings; multibow link bracelet; geometric crystal link bracelet with sapphire accents; crystal and sapphire swirl earrings.* Right-hand page, clockwise from upper left: *lorgnette of platinum and crystal; lorgnette with onyx-and-crystal handle; crystal link bracelet; crystal flower brooch with removable stem, inspired by a Harry Winston design; crystal snowflake pins; platinum earrings with pavé-set crystals.*

THE POWER OF COLOR
Three versions of a golden starburst cross brooch. Left: garnets, pearls, and crystals; top: topaz, crystal, and jet; right: emeralds, sapphires, and rubies.

BURSTS OF SPRING
Overleaf: Left-hand page, clockwise from upper left: *flower earrings with turquoise beading; crystal flower earrings with yellow and pink accents, each with matching brooch; golden "twig" brooch with coral center and crystal border; crystal bow earrings with detachable aquamarine drops; golden sunflower brooch and earrings with pavé-set crystals; turquoise egg earrings with crystal setting; pearl flower earrings with coral beading.* Right-hand page, clockwise from upper left: *three Maltese crosses of turquoise with peridot accents, coral with aquamarine accents, and ivory with tourmaline accents, plus matching earrings; coral cabochon earrings with crystals; golden "twin pin" with cut crystals, convertible to earrings; pearl button earrings with ivory and crystal; flower pin with multicolored crystal petals and crystal leaves.*

REGAL TREASURES

Clockwise from upper left: *double-strand pearl necklace with emerald and crystal clasp, plus coordinating earrings; pearl necklace with detachable cross pendant of emeralds and crystals, with pearl drop; clip earrings with rubies, crystals, and sapphires; double-strand pearl necklace with multicolored crystal rondelles; ruby brooch with crystals, emeralds, aquamarines, sapphires, tourmalines, and amethysts; cable bracelet with crystal, ruby, emerald, and sapphire endcaps; brooch with heart-shaped sapphire and pavé-set crystal starbursts; gold link bracelet with multicolor cabochon-cut posts and crystal accents; brooch with square- and oval-cut sapphires and crystal flowerettes; flower earrings with dome-cut rubies and pavé-set crystal petals.*

MESSAGES OF LOVE

Left to right: *chain charm bracelet with golden hearts and toggle clasp; "I Love You" link bracelet with pavé-set crystal details; chain necklace with interlocking crystal hearts; Victorian era–inspired necklace with "I Love You" coins; gold charm necklace with interchangeable heart pendants of pearl, crystal, and onyx on spring-ring clasp; heart pendant of fluted gold and pavé-set crystals, capped with a cabochon-cut ruby.*

VICTORIAN FANTASY

Overleaf: Left-hand page, clockwise from left: *golden cherub lorgnette; pendant with usable seal; black enamel brooch and removable drop, set with rubies and crystals; golden intaglio pendant on mesh chain; brooch with crystals and pink tourmalines; antiqued-gold cross earrings with seed pearls; heart-shaped pearl drop pin with enameled leaves.* Right-hand page, clockwise from upper left: *Victorian violet brooch and earrings of gold, amethyst, jade, and crystal; gold and enamel flower pin; amethyst brooch in golden setting; golden bee bracelet with pavé-set crystals; bracelet of ribbed-gold links and crystals; "eternal love" snake brooch with cushion-cut tourmaline center; "lovers' knot" pin with multitoned crystals.*

RENAISSANCE ARTISTRY

Clockwise from upper left: *necklace of rubies and emeralds; amethyst and emerald button earrings set in brushed gold, with crystal accents; multicolored intaglio bracelet with cabochon-tipped posts; ribbed-gold link bracelet with cabochon-cut lapis, jade, and carnelian; coordinating earrings of jade/ribbed lapis and lapis/ribbed tortoise; medieval cross pin with cabochon pearls and square-cut emeralds and rubies.*

MAGICAL MENAGERIE

Overleaf: Left-hand page, clockwise from upper left: *golden mama and baby bee pins with seed pearls, linked by a detachable chain; cable necklace with bees of gold, topaz, and black enamel; bee scatter pins pavé-set with rubies, amethysts, sapphires; crystal mama and baby bee pins; citrine mama and baby bee pins.* Center: *ribbed-gold beehive pin.* Right-hand page, clockwise from upper left: *double-strand pearl necklace with bee clasp; crystal mama and baby moth pins; bee pin with emeralds; crystal bee watch-pin; golden turtle watch-pin with seed pearls; movable teddy bear pin; Victorian-style birds-on-a-branch pin; ladybug pin of crystals, rubies, and black enamel; gold and crystal mama and baby turtle pins; Spike and Veronica in gold and jet, with removable chain; turtle link bracelet of gold, crystal, and cabochon-cut emeralds.*

WINDOWS TO THE PAST

Clockwise from upper left: *gold lorgnette with red- and black-enameled stem and laurel wreath detail; lorgnette of gold filigree on cable chain; long-stemmed lorgnette of malachite with rubies; Russian-style lorgnette enameled in tones of topaz and emerald, with crystal accents; gold lorgnette with pearl and crystal highlights; Art Deco–inspired lorgnette inset with tourmalines, sapphires, and crystals; Victorian-influenced lorgnette with stem of red enamel and pavé-set crystals; lorgnette with alabaster- and lapis-enameled stem bearing crest of Nicholas II, after a design by Fabergé; contemporary lorgnette with fluted-gold stem.*

GLAMOUR AND GLITTER

Overleaf: Clockwise from upper left: *double-strand pearl necklace with twin heart clasp in polished gold and pavé-set crystals; crystal heart earrings and pin set; quarter-moon brooch of pavé-set crystals; bracelet of polished gold and pavé-set crystal stars; crystal star earrings; snowflake scatter pins of gold with crystals; double-strand pearl necklace with crystal star clasp; pavé-set crystal fleur-de-lis brooch; golden rope chain with twirling crystal ball; gold balloon earrings with crystal details and pearl ends; four-leaf-clover pin of pavé-set crystals; crystal "Cupid's Arrow" pin; star-shaped scatter pins of crystal and gold.*

EARTH COLORS

Left-hand page, clockwise from upper left: *brown linked-pearl necklace; tortoise and ivory butterfly pins with gold and crystal accents; ivory flower pin with tortoise cabochons; topaz enamel earrings with gold braiding.* Right-hand page, clockwise from upper left: *gold link necklace with square-cut topaz and onyx and crystal detailing; tortoise earrings with crystal insets; gold earrings and pendant set with cushion-cut topaz; bracelet with amber and tortoise enamel; cabochon-cut tortoise button earrings.*

IMPERIAL SPLENDOR

Overleaf: Left-hand page, clockwise from upper left: *imperial eagle medallion and earrings of sapphire enamel with crystal and topaz; Fabergé-inspired egg brooch with crest of Nicholas II in enamel with crystals and seed pearls; Russian-inspired "Mother and Child" cameo brooch; crystal laurel-wreath earrings with square-cut rubies; gold and crystal crown earrings; hinged cuff bracelet of gold and crystal on blue enamel.* Right-hand page, clockwise from upper left: *Fabergé-inspired star sapphire brooch with crystal bow; heart-shaped lockets in ruby and sapphire enamel; golden picture-frame brooch with crystals and pearls; golden lorgnettes with enamel accents; balloon pins in rich, Russian-toned enamels.*

CLASSICAL CURRENCY

Clockwise from upper left: *linked gold choker with antique coin pendant encircled by crystals, plus matching earrings; golden mesh necklace with ancient coin motif; ribbed-gold earrings inset with pewter-toned coins and coordinating cuff bracelet.*

THE FEAST OF ST. PETERSBURG

Overleaf: Left-hand page, lower left: *golden egg-and-bow earrings and pendant set. Egg pendants, left to right: gold-wrapped crystal; emerald enamel with gold leaf-and-cross design; pavé-set rubies with golden bow; textured silver with golden bow; ladybug of black enamel, rubies, and crystals; black-diamond "caviar" egg; "Dearest" egg encircled with diamond, emerald, amethyst, ruby, emerald, sapphire, and topaz; pavé-set crystals with golden bow; sapphire enamel with crystal accents; white enamel, gold, crystal, cabochon-cut emerald; enamel Russian cross egg; seed pearls with golden bow; ruby enamel with gold leaf-and-cross design.* Right-hand page, left to right: *Fabergé-inspired egg and charm necklace with interchangeable eggs and charms of multicolored enamel, gold, pearls, and jade; chain necklace with gold-and-enamel eggs; interchangeable egg and charm earrings (shown with gold and pearl charms plus multicolored enamel eggs).*

BRIGHT BANGLES

Clockwise from upper left: *slim "stack" bangles inset with multicolor crystals; gold bangle bracelets with miracle-set crystal accents; bangles with multicolored crystal accents; hinged golden bangles with jewel-toned enamel and crystal insets; hinged rainbow bangle with cabochon-cut stones; hinged panther bracelet with a collar of emeralds, amethysts, topaz, and sapphires.*

GLEAMING GOLD, DRAMATIC BLACK

Overleaf: Left-hand page, left to right: *link bracelets of black enamel and gold; key necklace with intaglio; enamel bracelet with gold beading; cuff bracelet of gold, onyx, and crystal; pearl and jet brooch with crystals; jet and crystal Maltese cross with pearls and topaz; jet and pearl earrings with crystals.* Right-hand page, clockwise from upper left: *golden choker with onyx and crystals; oval pearl earrings with crystals and enamel; enamel and crystal cross earrings with pearls; heart locket of pavé-set jet and crystals; enamel bow earrings with crystal borders; jet, crystal, and amber cross earrings; hinged heart earrings of pavé-set jet and crystals.*

ALL THAT GLITTERS IS GOLDEN
Left-hand page, clockwise from upper left: *ribbed-gold bracelet with crystal-striped cylinders; egg-shaped, honeycomb-patterned earrings and locket of gold with crystals; deco-style flame earrings with pavé-set crystal borders; "Kisses" earrings of pavé-set crystal; deco flame brooch of gold and crystal.* Right-hand page, clockwise from upper left: *flexible gold cable bracelet with crystal barrel clasp; ribbed-gold "shell" bracelet with crystals; gold chain bracelet with crystal rondelles.*

DECO-DRAMA
Overleaf: Left-hand page, from left: *flower earrings of topaz and sapphires; open-link chain bracelet with square-cut crystals; golden mesh bracelet with rubies and sapphires; gold link bracelet with crystal accents; ribbed/polished gold link bracelet.* Right-hand page, clockwise from upper left: *gold ring with pavé-set crystals; flexible ribbed bracelet with crystal bands; polished gold bow pin with miracle-set crystals; quilted-look cuff bracelet with crystals; geometrical gold earrings with crystal accents; flower earrings of jade and carnelian cabochons.*

CITY GOLD

Left-hand page, left to right: *basket-weave cuff bracelet of brushed gold; comedy and tragedy pins; golden knot earrings; open-link chain necklace; triple-chain bracelet.* Right-hand page, left to right: *flexible ribbed-gold choker; multi-strand golden bead necklace; gold choker with barrel clasp.*

JEWEL TONES

Overleaf: Left-hand page, clockwise from upper left: *heart pendant of amethyst enamel; bangle bracelet of marquise-cut amethysts; ivory enamel bangle bracelet; bracelet of sapphire and emerald enamel on gold; earrings in emerald and sapphire enamel with gold details; sapphire enamel ring with pavé-set crystal center; sapphire enamel earrings with crystal borders; ivory enamel earrings with gold cross-hatching.* Right-hand page, clockwise from upper left: *hinged serpent bracelet in blue enamel with gold patterning and crystal details; ruby enamel bow with pavé-set crystal border; chain bracelet with red and black enamel ladybug clasp, and matching earrings; lovers' knot brooch of sapphire enamel with gold and crystal ribbons; cherry pin of red enamel fruit and gold/crystal leaves; circle/ribbon pin in emerald enamel with crystals.* Center: *lapis enamel earrings with gold cross-hatching.*

SLY METAMORPHOSIS

Clockwise from upper left: *bolo-style necklace with interchangeable tips of jet, pearl, and tortoise; hinged gold bracelet with removable end caps of pearl/sapphire/ruby, pearl/black enamel, amethyst/red enamel, pavé-set crystal; button earrings with magnetized centers of ivory, tortoise, onyx; deco watch with strap options of black leather, triple-strand pearls, gold link mesh; gold ring with magnetized centers of pearl, jet; hoop earrings with detachable charms of gold, jet, pearl, crystal; door-knocker earrings with removable disks of onyx, ivory, lapis, tortoise, malachite, amethyst; gold filigree egg pendant with removable eggs; pendant with interchangeable ends of jet, lapis, tortoise, gold tassel, and pearl heart. Center: gold and crystal flower pin, convertible to earrings.*

FOREVER PEARLS

Overleaf: *An extravagance of pale jewels, including, from left, pavé-set crystal bow earrings; gold filigree lorgnette; square pearl pendant with pearl drop, convertible to brooch; open-strand necklace of 12-mm pearls with crystal-topped tassel ends; tassel earrings with pearls and pavé-set crystals; square-cut pearl button earrings; and a cuff bracelet of pearl and pavé-set flowerettes in a checkerboard pattern. Underneath it all, a ten-foot pearl necklace.*

THE CLASSICS COLLECTION ❧ 133

TIMELESS ELEGANCE

Left to right: *pendant watch with black dial and black enamel frame on gold chain with jet beads; dress watch with dial and bracelet of gold and pavé-set crystals; "panther-link" bracelet watch with sliding pavé-set crystal bezel; gold "panther-link" bracelet watch with black dial and crystal markers; four-strand pearl and gold beaded bracelet watch with mother-of-pearl dial; gold and black beaded bracelet watch with crystal-accented black dial; ribbed-silver bangle watch; quilted-gold cuff watch with expandable band; charm necklace with lobster-claw clasp, shown with gold charms (clover, bee, elephant) and gold lorgnette, gold and pearl heart pendant, moon and star pendant with crystal details, and gold pendant watch with black dial and crystal markers; gold and silver link bracelet watch.*

Some people believe that "high-quality costume jewelry" is a contradiction in terms, but I'm not one of them. Every piece of jewelry, whether it's "real" or not, should be so well made that it can survive years of active service, then be passed along from generation to generation. Am I an idealist? Absolutely. But I'm also a realist, and in my years of collecting I have learned that fine jewelry incorporates three basic elements: good design; strong, long-lasting materials; and excellent craftsmanship. You'll notice that nowhere in this formula does the word *precious* appear. Because, although diamonds and rubies may contribute significantly to the cost of a piece, they don't necessarily guarantee its quality.

A finished piece of jewelry from the Joan Rivers Classics Collection is readied for shipping.

FINE AND FAUX: THE MEANING OF QUALITY

Let me give you an example. Say you inherit an emerald brooch from your grandmother's estate. Certainly the stones are valuable, and so, presumably, is your sentimental attachment to the heirloom. But if that brooch catches on your clothing or has a clasp that's impossible to operate, what are you going to do with it? Stash it in a safe place and visit it once a year, that's what. Often, women who own expensive yet poorly designed pieces will wrestle with ancestral guilt, then eventually end up having the stones refashioned into something they'll wear and enjoy.

There's a happier example on the other side of that coin. Imagine going through your great-aunt's jewel box and finding a brooch that you absolutely adore. Do you care that it's made from faux stones, that it didn't cost a fortune in its day? Not a whit. You'll cherish it and think of your wonderful auntie every time you wear it. I myself have a necklace from eighteenth-century France that I'm crazy about, made from what they used to call "cheap paste." In its time it was an inexpensive bauble, but to me it's more real than real. I love it for its beauty, its style, and the wonderful patina it's acquired with the passage of time. I also recognize that, long ago in some Parisian workshop, skilled artisans and craftspeople labored long and hard over that necklace. They set each stone with care, they fashioned links and clasps that would stand the test of time.

When I think about quality, I'm often reminded of Coco Chanel. Coco, you know, was a woman of legendary style. She owned a spectacular collection of jewelry, and also kept *copies* of her favorite pieces. When she stepped out, that sly minx would mix and match the real and the fake, so that no one was quite sure whether she was wearing a million dollars worth of pearls or a hundred dollars worth of glass. Coco was a brilliant designer, you understand, so she knew better than anyone that jewelry's fashion impact comes not from carat weight but from color, drape, line, form, fit, wit, and meticulous craftsmanship — the very qualities I strive for when creating each piece in the Joan Rivers Classics Collection.

MODELS, CASTINGS, GOOD VIBRATIONS . . . AND A WHITE-GLOVE FINISH

It's not easy to manufacture high-quality jewelry while keeping the cost within human reach. In fact, when I first got started in the jewelry business, numerous well-meaning experts told me that my vision was unrealistic. But instead of taking "no" for an answer, David and I rolled up our sleeves and learned everything we could about the manufacturing process. We visited Providence, Rhode Island, where most of the country's costume jewelry is made (including mine). We pestered designers, model makers, and suppliers until we *found* ways to get the pieces we wanted at the prices we wanted. Though we started as amateurs, somewhere along the way we became experts — and both of us became fascinated with the intricate process that is required to take a piece of jewelry from start to finish.

All jewelry begins with an idea. I might see something that captures my imagination — the pattern on a piece of fabric, an architectural detail, a combination of colors — and away I go. First, I do a rough sketch. Let me emphasize *rough:* I've done preliminary drawings on cocktail napkins and carried them to Providence in my purse. There, I get together with a designer. I've learned the hard way that the more details you can work out on paper, the more time and money you save in production later on. So when I collaborate with a designer, we work back and forth until what I see in my head is realized in a full-color rendering.

The second step involves something called an "accurate" — a technical drawing of a piece of jewelry and its various components. In making an accurate, a designer has got to be part engineer and part artist,

Left: *In the beginning, there's an idea. Here, a designer turns one of my rough sketches into a full-color rendering.*

Right: *If you look carefully at this photo, you'll see an artist's rendering (lower left); a "hand model" (upper left); an "accurate" paired with a finished, polished product (center); plus an assortment of white-metal samples (lower right). Also pictured are some of the tools of the model-making trade.*

because he or she is responsible for creating a bridge between vision and reality. For example, if I present an artist's rendering of, shall we say, a drop earring, the designer will come up with separate drawings of the drop, the link, and the wire, and each of these components will be shown from the front, from the back, and in profile — all in perfect scale. Talk about precise! The accurates have got to be perfect, because they will be used by the model makers as a guide.

Model making is an intricate, labor-intensive phase. Each model is like a tiny sculpture, hand-carved from a soft base-metal alloy or wax. It can take twelve to fourteen hours to produce the model for a simple button earring, so a piece with five or six components can take as many as forty hours. Since the model, called a "hand model," represents what the final product will look like, I usually examine it carefully. If it passes my inspection, craftspeople get to work creating a "white-metal" sample, that is, a sample made from a harder metal that hasn't yet been gold

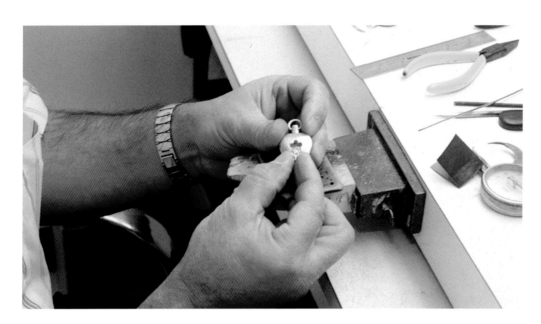

The telltale heart. A Rhode Island craftsman fits a flower-shaped setting into a model of a heart-shaped pendant; faux pearls will eventually fill the five indentations.

plated. At this point in production, final changes can be made. If I don't love a particular stone or a particular element of the design, I send it back for adjustments.

Next comes commitment. For some people commitment is almost impossible. For me it's easy: when everything is absolutely perfect, and I've decided that the white-metal casting represents the very piece of jewelry that I can't live without, the starting whistle is blown and production begins.

Production molds are what finished pieces of jewelry are cast from. Dozens of identical molds are encased in a wheel of hard rubber. These wheels are stacked inside a large drum for a process called "spin casting" — which, by the way, should never be confused with what one does on a fishing trip. Instead, picture a molten metal being poured into a funnel at the top of a drum. Inside the closed drum, the miniature carousels spin on an axis, while centrifugal action forces liquid metal into the nooks and crannies of each mold. Once cooled, those metal-filled production molds are removed from the drum and the rubber is broken away. The resulting wheels still look like miniature carousels, only now they're made from hardened metal.

When a piece of jewelry emerges from the spin-casting process, it's rather a mess. Stray pieces of metal stick out of visible seams, and the metal itself is lumpish and rough. Now the cleaning and finishing can begin. First, craftspeople liberate the individual pieces from the casting wheel, using small knives to carve away the most obvious imperfections. Then, each piece of future jewelry is immersed in a machine filled with little beads. When the machine is turned on it performs a violent shimmy, and all those beads vibrate against the rough metal and make it smooth,

Top left: *Nine perfect prototypes are prepared for the casting process.*

Top right: *Is it soup yet? This cauldron is called a spin caster. Inside, a stack of identical circular molds is being filled with a molten metal alloy.*

Bottom left: *Future pendants, still attached to cooled circles of raw metal, are broken out of their hard rubber molds.*

Bottom right: *Here's where the real fun begins. Those pink triangles may look like a sea of Valentine's Day candies, but actually they're polishing beads inside a vibratory machine. Those beads will shimmy and shake against the metal pendant until it loses its rough edges, a process called "vibing."*

smoother, smoothest. The process, called "vibing," must be carefully timed so that each piece acquires a silken surface but doesn't lose its fine detail. When it's just right, it's then hand-finished on a polishing wheel to a blinding shine.

Next comes plating. Plating is that delicious process in which a piece is dipped in sterling silver or, more often, 24-karat gold. It's amazing to watch, because as many as five hundred pieces of jewelry can be attached to a rack and plated all at once. Imagine seeing mere metal turn to shining gold, just like that! It's like a high-tech fairy tale come true.

Of course, the most visually dramatic step involves the setting of stones. Believe it or not, every single stone in every single piece of my jewelry is set by hand. That's a lot of work, even when an earring or necklace design features only one stone. Can you imagine the labor that goes into a pavé-set piece, like my glittering star pin? Hundreds of faceted, hand-cut crystals must be positioned and glued, one at a time.

Last, but certainly not least, every piece of finished jewelry must go through inspection and be packed. This is usually done by workers wearing white gloves. They examine each piece, wipe it so it's pristine and gleaming, then pack it into a gift box.

Right: *When a skilled craftsman meets a high-speed polishing machine, the result is a blindingly beautiful shine.*

Below: *Everybody in the pool! These pieces, delicately wired on a frame, are being electroplated with 24-karat gold.*

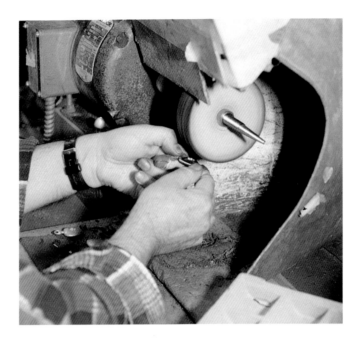

Facing page, left: *Each stone on each piece of my jewelry must be individually set. Here, tiny crystals are placed, one at a time, in a pavé setting.*

Facing page, right: *The inspection has been made, and the finished product is examined one last time.*

What reaches the consumer at home is the result of hundreds of hours of caring, loving labor. Is it all worth it? Oh, yes. Whenever I hear that one of my pieces has been handed down from mother to daughter, I am both moved and proud; it confirms my conviction that beauty is eternal and quality is priceless.

Shopping Tips

You say some bright bijou has caught your eye? That's wonderful, exciting — but before you put money on the counter, spend a little time checking for quality. First, turn that piece of jewelry over in your hand and examine the back. Are there any rough spots that may snag your favorite sweater or irritate your delicate skin? The back of any piece, whether it's a pin, a necklace, earrings, a bracelet, a watch, or a ring, should be utterly smooth and blemish-free. Nobody will see the back but you, of course, but *you're* the one who's going to wear it. And that's rule number one: When shopping for jewelry, remember that you're the most important person in the world. More tips to ease your way:

EARRINGS

If you've got sensitive lobes, weight is important when choosing earrings. Considering a clip? Make sure it doesn't squeeze your earlobe. If your ears are pierced, don't buy anything that's heavy enough to visibly pull your lobes down.

NECKLACES

The fit of a necklace is of utmost importance. A choker should rest against your neck, without gaps or squeezes, while link necklaces should lie flat all the way around your collarbone and your chest. In all cases, make sure a necklace is comfortable against the back of your neck; is smooth enough not to catch or snag fine fabrics; and features a clasp that is easy for you to operate.

PINS/BROOCHES

Maybe you're mad for that beautiful brooch — but if it flops forward when you pin it on your lapel, just say *nyet!* Likewise, a pin shouldn't be so heavy that it pulls down on your clothing. And always be sure that your pin features a clasp that you can open and close without performing major acrobatics.

BRACELETS/WATCHES

Bangle bracelets, chain bracelets, and watchbands of a loose bracelet design should all hang about a quarter inch away from your wrist. If you're shopping for a bracelet that fits flush against your wrist, such as a cuff bracelet, make sure it fits snugly, but not tightly. If you have trouble with clasps, look for a toggle design; these are easily negotiated with one hand.

RINGS

Obviously, a ring should be tight enough to stay on, but not so tight that it requires soaping to remove. A less-obvious consideration involves the wearing of gloves; remember that in winter, you may have to choose between freezing hands and that hunk of ice on your finger.

I could talk about jewelry forever (and probably would, if anyone would let me). But when all has been said about the history, symbolism, and aesthetics of my favorite subject, the details add up to one simple truth: Jewelry makes us look good and feel good. I'm sure Eve chose the most attractive fig leaf when she and Adam were kicked out of the Garden of Eden, and in our modern lives we need jewelry more than ever. As we work hard and play hard in a thousand different roles, jewelry is there for us to love and enjoy, to boost our spirits, and to make us feel that anything is possible.

The Joan Rivers Classics Collection has been a delight to design, and it's been my pleasure to present this book of jewels to you. I hope you enjoy owning, reading, and just gazing at it as much as I've enjoyed creating it for you.

Remember, life is short. Treat yourself right, and go for the glamour!

Love,

Joan Rivers

BIBLIOGRAPHY

Fregnac, Claude. *Jewelry from the Renaissance to Art Nouveau.* London: Octopus Books, 1973.

Habsburg, Géza von, and Marina Lopato. *Fabergé: Imperial Jeweller.* London: Thames and Hudson, 1993.

Krashes, Laurence S. *Harry Winston: The Ultimate Jeweler.* New York and Santa Monica, Calif.: Harry Winston, Inc. and the Gemological Institute of America, 1993.

Nadelhoffer, Hans. *Cartier: Jewelers Extraordinary.* New York: Harry N. Abrams, 1984.

Munn, Geoffrey C. *The Triumph of Love: Jewelry 1530–1930.* London: Thames and Hudson, 1993.

Snowman, A. Kenneth. *Carl Fabergé: Goldsmith to the Imperial Court of Russia.* London: Debrett's Peerage Limited, 1980.

———. *Fabergé: Lost and Found: The Recently Discovered Jewelry Designs from the St. Petersburg Archives.* New York: Harry N. Abrams, 1993.

———, ed. *The Master Jewelers.* New York: Harry N. Abrams, 1990.

Von Solodkoff, Alexander, Roy D. R. Betteley, Paul Schaffer, A. Kenneth Snowman, and Marilyn Pfeifer Swezey. *Masterpieces from the House of Fabergé.* New York: Harry N. Abrams, 1984.

INDEX *(Italic page numbers refer to illustrations.)*